This is a story about a rea
over one thousand years

It was a cold night in winter.
King Alfred was lost in the forest.
He saw a little house.
He knocked on the door.

1

A woman came out.
She had flour on her hands.
Alfred could smell baking.
"May I have some food?" he asked.

Alfred looked tired and dirty.
The woman did not know he was the King.
"Sit by the fire," she said.
"Watch my cakes for me and
be sure they don't burn."

The woman went out to feed her pigs.
Alfred was so tired he fell asleep.
He began to dream.
He dreamt of the hall he had lived in
with his family when he was a boy.

He dreamt of the dark nights when his
mother would read to them.
She read stories and poems from
a special book.
The letters were painted red, blue and gold.

His mother had said, "I will give this book to the child who is the first to learn the poems." Alfred could not read, but he could remember all the poems.

Then Alfred dreamt of the Vikings.
The Vikings came from across the sea.
They killed many people and stole everything.

When Alfred grew up he helped
his father fight the Vikings.
Then his father was killed.
Alfred was made King.

Alfred heard the noise of
battle in his dreams.
He smelled burning.
The Vikings tried to catch him but
he ran into the forest.

He remembered that he was lost and
could not find his men.
Then... he remembered the cakes!
The woman finished feeding the pigs.
"My cakes are burnt!" she shouted.

She hit the King over the head.

Alfred heard men calling his name.
The door opened and in came Alfred's men.
"The King!" they shouted.
"We have found the King!"

"Now it is time to fight!" said Alfred.
"We must go and find the Vikings."
He thanked the woman and went
away with his men.

When they met the Vikings there
was a terrible battle.
Alfred's men won.

But Alfred did not kill the Vikings.
He said, "We must not fight any more."
Alfred and the Vikings made peace.

Alfred was a very good king.
He remembered the book his mother
had read when he was a little boy.
He built schools for the children so
they could learn to read books too.